Exposing Mega Churches and the Prosperity Gospel Scam
They Could Feed Every Starving Person Worldwide and House Every American

Henry Bechthold

Contents

Mega Churches and Mega Money 1

Prosperity Gospel Biblically Refuted 11

Prosperity Gospel Heresy and Blasphemy...............23

Prosperity Gospel—Does Everyone Get Healed? 55

Mega Churches and Mega Money

It should deeply bother and concern every Christian that millions of people will die from starvation this year, and that hundreds of thousands of Americans are homeless, while Christian churches and ministries in America have enough money in their bank and investment accounts to feed all of these starving people three meals a day throughout the year, and to also house, feed, job train and provide medical care for every homeless person in America.

Today's Christian Church in America has become a gigantic commercial enterprise. There are thousands of mega churches throughout the United States, with most of them ranging in price from ten million to one hundred million dollars each. And, per the National Center for Charitable Statistics (NCCS), in 2011 American Christian churches and ministries received **$174,000,000,000** in donations/offerings. Because there are a lot of "zeros" in that number, which can be a bit confusing, I will restate that number in words. American Christian churches and ministries had an income of **one hundred, seventy-four billion dollars** in 2011. And, because this number tends to increase most years, that figure is probably closer to two hundred billion by now.

The amount of the Church's income is not the concern, but rather what they are spending their money on: huge, extravagant church facilities and ministry buildings with *state-of-the-art* equipment and luxurious furnishings, church and ministry owned private jets costing from a few million to twenty million dollars each, multimillion dollar homes provided for church pastors and ministry preachers, church and ministry owned luxury automobiles each costing up to $100,000 or more, and preacher's salaries ranging in the hundreds of thousands of dollars. All of this being done while millions of people are dying from starvation each year throughout the world, and hundreds of thousands of Americans are homeless. And, as previously stated, while these American churches and ministries have the money to feed every one of those starving people three meals a day throughout the year, and to house, feed and provide medical care for America's entire homeless population. This is an outrage, and it is **not** "what Jesus would do"!

Of course, those in the Church who are spending their donated funds on all of these "material things" are quick to justify their actions. They remind us that the Jewish temple in the Old Testament also was an extremely expensive and luxurious building. Unfortunately, their comparison and reasoning are both quite faulty. If they really want to compare their modern churches to the temple, the first thing they should do is to close all of their coffee shops, bookstores, arcade rooms and restaurants that they have included in their expensive church facilities. Why? Because the Bible states that Jesus cast the "sellers" and "money changers" out of the temple, and He said that we are not to make His Father's house, a "house of merchandise", in John 2:16 and Matthew 21:12. In other words, do not turn the temple into a "place of business". Therefore, if today's church leaders want to compare their buildings with the temple, then their profitable bookstores, restaurants, amusement rooms and coffee shops need to be eliminated. However, it is highly unlikely that you will be seeing this occur anytime soon. You see, the contemporary Church does not want to conduct itself like the Old Testament temple when it comes to reverence and sanctity, but only when it comes to expensive and luxurious adornment.

It is also noteworthy, that the Jewish temple housed the "Most Holy Place" with the Shekinah Glory, the *Ark of the Covenant,* the tablets of stone with the Ten Commandments written by God, the "mercy seat" and other divinely appointed objects. It was so holy that only the high priest could enter it, and just once each year.

On the other hand, in Jesus' day, there were numerous synagogues throughout the land, in which the common people worshipped on a weekly basis; they were very ordinary structures. Those synagogues would be the equivalent of our churches today, **and not the temple.**

As previously stated, the leaders of today's wealthy and worldly churches want to compare their structures to the temple, in order to justify their luxurious buildings. Thus, we are ending up with thousands of *temples* throughout America, while the *commonplace churches* are quickly vanishing from the American landscape.

Christian leaders have conveniently forgotten that there was only "one" temple in all of Israel, while there were numerous modest synagogues throughout the land. God didn't need *thousands of temples* in the land of Israel, and it is likely that He doesn't need them in America either.

Many ministries and mega churches will show some of their humanitarian ministries, such as feeding starving children in some third world country, to give the impression that they give a large percentage of their income to these types of causes. They may show that they gave $100,000 to charitable causes in a given year, which sounds quite impressive. It sounds impressive until you realize that their income was $20 million for that year, which means that their donations towards charitable causes were only one-half of one percent of their income. It sounds impressive until you realize that the preacher's salary alone was several times greater than the total amount given towards these charitable causes. I will be discussing these "prosperity preachers" and their unfathomable wealth and profligate lifestyle a little later. You will be shocked at what is going on in this "prosperity gospel".

One of the most common slogans in Christianity is, "What would Jesus do"? It would be a good idea for today's Church to ask itself this question. The Jesus we read about in the Bible spent His life ministering to people's needs, not ministering to Himself. I think it is reasonable to assume that He would ask His Church to follow His personal example, by also ministering to those in need, instead of ministering to itself. As the Scriptures state in 1st John 2:6, we are to "walk" as He (Jesus) "walked"; that is, we are to live our lives patterned after the example of Jesus' life revealed in the Bible. And, regarding ministering to others, in Matthew 25:31-46, Jesus taught that true Christianity is manifested in feeding the hungry, clothing the naked and ministry in general to those in need. This is what Christian churches and ministries should be doing, not ministering to themselves.

It is both astonishing and disturbing to realize what America's Christian churches and ministries could accomplish if they dedicated just a fraction of their annual income to "real ministry". According to the United Nations, about 7.6 million people die from starvation, malnutrition and other hunger related diseases each year. And, per World Hunger.org, nearly six million of these are children. The "Feed My Starving Children" ministry organization states that it costs less than 25 cents to provide one nourishing meal; other ministry websites and organizations say that a nourishing meal can be provided at a cost of just 20 cents. However, even if you use the higher figure of 25 cents per meal, this means that, for just 75 cents a day, three nourishing meals can be provided for one starving person. When you multiply 75 cents per day times 365 days in a year, you arrive at a figure of $273.75 to provide three nourishing meals every day throughout the year to a starving person. Then when you multiply that $273.75 amount times the 7.6 million people who die from starvation and malnutrition each year, you arrive at a figure of $2,080,500,000 (two billion, eighty million, five hundred thousand dollars) to provide three nourishing meals to every starving person in the world each and every day throughout the year. This "$2,080,500,000" figure equals just 1.2% of the $174 billion income of Christian churches and ministries reported in 2011, and would probably be an even smaller percentage based on 2020 figures. Do you think that America's wealthy Christian churches and ministries could afford to spend 1.2% of their massive income to feed every starving person in the world three meals a day throughout the year?

According to Wikipedia and other websites that provide homeless statistics, there are 554,000 homeless people in America on any given night. And, per a recent study done by "Creative Housing Solutions", an Oklahoma based consultants group, and reported on the "Think Progress.org" website, $10,051 per year would provide housing, job training and health care for a homeless person. When you multiply that $10,051 amount times the 554,000 people who are homeless on any given night in America, you arrive at a figure of $5,568,254,000 (five billion, five hundred sixty-eight million, two hundred fifty-four thousand dollars) annually to house, job train, and provide medical care for every homeless person in America. You can then add on three nourishing meals a day throughout the year for each homeless person at a total cost of $151,657,500, which increases the grand total to $5,719,911,500. This grand total figure, which would provide housing, three meals a day, health care and job training for all of the 554,000 people who are homeless on any given night in America, equals just 3.3% of the $174 billion income of American Christian churches and ministries reported in 2011, and would probably be an even smaller percentage based on 2020 figures. Do you think that America's wealthy Christian churches and ministries could afford to spend 3.3% of their massive income to resolve America's homeless problem; getting the homeless off the streets and providing for their needs?

When you add the $2,080,500,000 amount that would feed the starving, to the $5,719,911,500 amount that would provide for America's homeless population, you arrive at a total amount of $7,800,411,500, which equals less than 4.5% of the $174 billion annual income of America's Christian churches and ministries, based on 2011 figures. Even if the various numbers reported from the organizations and websites that I've cited are somewhat inaccurate, even if the actual numbers should be twice as high; that would still only amount to less than 9% of the annual income of Christian churches and ministries in America. Is not preventing the starvation of 7.6 million people annually, and housing and providing for the needs of the hundreds of thousands of homeless Americans, more important than building luxurious churches and ministry buildings, than purchasing private jets and luxury automobiles, than building multimillion dollar homes for preachers, and than paying "fat cat" CEO type six figure salaries to ministers?

It literally sickens and angers me to see the selfishness, materialism and "luxurious living" within so much of the Christian Church in America, while millions of people die from starvation annually, and while America's homeless population lives in cardboard boxes and eats out of garbage cans. This is **not** *what Jesus would do*! This is **not** biblical Christianity! This is the conducting of a profitable, religious "business enterprise", and masquerading it as Christian ministry.

Jesus spent His life ministering to those in need. And, the Bible states, in 1st John 3:17-18, that if we see others in need, but do not help them, the love of God does not abide in us. It is time for the Church to practice what it preaches, or else to stop preaching.

Chapter Two

Prosperity Gospel Biblically Refuted

There is another "outrage" taking place in Christian churches and ministries throughout America. What is it? It is a "false gospel", a *prosperity wealth and health gospel*, being proclaimed by "prosperity preachers". What is this prosperity gospel? It is a doctrine that teaches Christians that if they have strong faith and "sow a financial seed", give an offering, into a church or ministry that proclaims the *prosperity gospel*, they will receive a "harvest" of good health and wealth from God. This "prosperity doctrine" proudly and unashamedly assures people that the devil cannot harm their health or finances as long as they maintain this strong faith and keep sowing those financial seeds. Therefore, according to these prosperity preaching organizations, all "contributing" Christians with strong faith are guaranteed to be healthy and wealthy. This results in a selfish "giving money to get blessings" mentality.

It's too bad that these contemporary "prosperity preachers", with their supposed great faith, are not able to go to many of the third world countries where impoverished Christians suffer from various diseases due to poor living conditions and lack of medicine, and who are also being beaten, imprisoned and martyred for their faith. Evidently these poverty stricken Christians, who are being maimed and killed for their faith in Jesus, must not have had the great faith of these American churches and ministries who proclaim this prosperity message. Also, the Apostle Paul, who wrote about half of the New Testament, must not have had as great of faith as these modern "prosperity preachers" either, because he said that he and the other apostles were hungry, poorly clothed and homeless, in 1st Corinthians 4:9-11. In fact, even Jesus must not have had a faith as great as these prosperity preaching ministers, because He said that even foxes and birds had homes, but He had no place to lay His head, in Matthew 8:20; in other words,

Jesus was also homeless. If only today's prosperity preaching churches and ministries in America could have instructed Paul and Jesus about having strong faith and "sowing financial seeds", perhaps they could have lived their lives with greater faith and comfort. Of course, this is untrue and absurd, as is the prosperity gospel being preached today. However, this teaching is seductive, and churches and ministries who promote this doctrine are growing rapidly. With this teaching you can have the best of both worlds. Now you can be a Christian, but not have to deny self anymore. Now you can be a Christian, but still enjoy all the things of the world. In fact, with this "prosperity gospel", being a Christian will guarantee you wealth and health!

It used to be that Christianity was known for the "cross" of self-sacrifice. In Matthew 16:24, Jesus told His disciples that anyone who wanted to follow Him would have to deny himself and take up his cross. However, prosperity preaching Christian churches and ministries have come up with a *new and improved tactic* for recruiting disciples. They have decided to allow prospective disciples to *trade up* from a "cross" to a "Cadillac". Instead of asking for self-denial, as Jesus did, they promise the pampering of self with rewards of wealth and health for giving to God. Of course, the way that you give to God is by giving to their churches and ministries. Some even go so far as to promise a hundredfold return from God on the donations made to their ministries. And, many of these "prosperity gospel" churches and ministries try to justify their unbiblical and worldly conduct by even suggesting that Jesus, His disciples, and the Apostle Paul were also wealthy themselves.

Well, what about this prosperity gospel? Does it square with Scripture? Were Jesus and Paul wealthy? As previously mentioned, Jesus said, in Matthew 8:20, that foxes and birds had homes, but He Himself had nowhere to lay His head; Jesus was homeless. And, as also mentioned previously, the Apostle Paul stated that he and his fellow apostles were hungry, thirsty, poorly clothed, and homeless, in 1st Corinthians 4:9-11. Moreover, Jesus said that His disciples would also *live lives of self-denial and sacrifice*, taking up their "cross", in Matthew 10:38; Matthew 16:24; Mark 8:34; Luke 9:23; Luke 14:27 and Luke 14:33. The preceding scriptures portray a completely different lifestyle than what is presented by prosperity preachers. Jesus also said, in Matthew 6:19-21 and Matthew 6:24, that we are *not to lay up treasures on this Earth*, but in Heaven; furthermore, that we cannot serve two masters, God and money. However, prosperity preachers contradict Jesus by encouraging their audiences to believe for and to expect worldly treasures as a reward for their great faith. But the Bible states, in James 4:4 and 1st John 2:15, that if we are attached to and love this world and "its things", *we are enemies of God and do not have His love in us*. Do you think that prosperity preachers with their diamond rings, Rolex watches, expensive designer clothing, multiple luxury automobiles, multimillion dollar homes and private jets might qualify as loving this world and its things? Who are you going to trust and obey, Jesus and the Scriptures, or prosperity preachers who contradict Him and His Word?

Whereas prosperity preachers present their wealth as being proof of their strong faith, their closeness to God, and as being a blessing that God will bestow upon all Christians who have strong faith; Jesus presents a completely opposite picture. He stated that it is "hard" for *rich people* to enter Heaven, in Matthew 19:23, Mark 10:23 and Luke 18:24. Furthermore, Jesus stressed the "danger" of *riches* in His parable of the *sower of the seed*, when He said that God's Word is ***choked*** by the "deceitfulness of riches", in Mark 4:19 and Luke 8:14. Thus, these prosperity preachers are encouraging people to desire and strive for the very thing that will make it harder for them to enter Heaven, and that will potentially ***choke*** God's word in them. Moreover, whereas prosperity preachers tell Christians to desire and strive for wealth, and to expect material riches to result from a strong faith; the Bible declares that those who hasten to be rich will not go "unpunished", in Proverbs 28:20. The Scriptures also state that people who desire to be rich fall into temptation and a snare; warning that they fall into foolish and harmful lusts that lead them to destruction and perdition, per 1st Timothy 6:9. And, rather than proclaiming money to be a reward or a proof of strong faith, Scripture warns that the love of money is the root of all evil, in 1st Timothy 6:10. Furthermore, while prosperity preachers proudly speak of their luxurious homes, cars, yachts and private jets as being proof of their "status with God", Jesus states, in Luke 12:16-21, that it is ***"fools" who lay up treasures for themselves***. Therefore, per Jesus, today's prosperity preachers are "fools", and **not** men of God.

I find it interesting that *prosperity preachers* tell Christians that a strong, abundant, rich faith will result in them being financially rich, while they tell them that they will remain *poor* if they do not have this strong, abundant, rich faith. However, the Bible says that it is the **poor** who are "rich in faith", in James 2:5.

The truth of the matter is that today's popular "prosperity gospel" blatantly contradicts Scripture. Prosperity preachers are manipulating and twisting Scripture to keep the money coming in, so that they can continue living lavishly. As the Apostle Paul said in 2nd Corinthians 2:17, in the New King James Version, there are "so many" who **peddle** the word of God. Keep in mind that Paul also said, in 2nd Timothy 3:13, that *evil men and "impostors" will grow worse and worse, deceiving and being deceived.* So, if there were already *so many* "peddling" the word of God in Paul's day, we can expect that there will be many more doing so today.

Per the Strong's Expanded Exhaustive Concordance, the Greek word translated as "peddle", in 2nd Corinthians 2:17, is "kapeleuo", which is from the Greek word "kapelos", which, according to Strongs', means a **huckster**. And, in fact, the

Amplified Bible does include the word, "huckster", in their translation of this verse, which follows.

"For we are not, like so many, [like **hucksters** making a trade of] peddling God's word [shortchanging and adulterating the divine message]".

And, the Amplified Bible obviously got their translation of this passage correct because, the Strong's Expanded Exhaustive Concordance provides the following commentary about this Greek word used in 2nd Corinthians 2:17: "This word means to be a retailer, to peddle, to "**hucksterize**"; hence, intentionally to get base gain by dealing in anything, to do anything for sordid personal advantage." This is a perfect description of today's prosperity preachers who manipulate and twist scriptures to obtain donations intended to preach the gospel of Jesus Christ, and then use large portions of these donations to purchase multimillion dollar homes, multiple luxury automobiles worth hundreds of thousands of dollars, private jets ranging from a few million dollars to twenty million dollars, and to pay themselves huge six figure salaries. All of this while millions of children are dying from starvation and hundreds of thousands of Americans are homeless.

For quite some time I have been referring to these prosperity preachers, with their diamond rings, Rolex watches, designer suits and ties, cosmetic surgeries, and other previously mentioned multimillion dollar "toys", as being "hucksters", without realizing that the Amplified Bible translation and the Strong's Expanded Exhaustive Concordance also use the word *huckster or hucksterize* for those who "peddle" the word of God.

Famous contemporary prosperity preachers such as Kenneth Copeland, Jesse Duplantis, Benny Hinn, Joel Osteen, Creflo Dollar and Joyce Meyer have "net worths" *conservatively* ranging from $8 million to $300 million. They have private jets ranging from a few million dollars to $20 million. Some of them have multiple private jets. They live in multimillion dollar homes that are many thousands of square feet in size; one of them being 35,000 square feet. Some of them have multiple multimillion dollar houses. And, some of them also own luxury yachts. Each one of them owns multiple luxury automobiles worth hundreds of thousands of dollars; brand names like Rolls Royce, Maserati, Ferrari, Porsche, Mercedes, etc.. One of them owns a $260,000 Maserati, and another owns a $350,000 Rolls Royce.

Haven't these prosperity preachers ever heard of automobile brands like Ford, Buick, Dodge, Toyota or Honda? Cadillac isn't even good enough for these hucksters. Why don't they purchase a luxury Ford, Toyota or Honda for $50,000, instead of a $350,000 Rolls Royce, and then use the $300,000 they would have saved to feed 1100 starving children three meals a day for a full year? Mr. Copeland, why not use that $20 million you spent on a *second* private jet, to instead feed nearly 64,000 starving children three meals a day for a full year? Which do you think Jesus would do, buy the Rolls Royce and the second jet, or feed the starving children?

You can go on Google and pull up video clips of Jesse Duplantis stating that Jesus told him to purchase another private jet; this one costing $54 million. You can also pull up video clips of Creflo Dollar declaring that Jesus told him to purchase another private jet as well, costing $65 million. I guess Jesus must love Creflo $11 million more than He loves Jesse. Seriously, do you think that Jesus actually told Jesse and Creflo to purchase these jets totaling $119 million, when that amount of money could feed 434,703 starving children three meals a day for an entire year?

Just the interest income from Joyce Meyer's and Kenneth Copeland's $10 million and $20 million private jets would purchase them a few hundred "first class" plane tickets each year to get them to their speaking engagements. However, Joyce Meyer once stated that all of the hassles of going through commercial airports *wore her out*, but now her private jet allows her to arrive at her meetings "fresh". Wow, I wonder how "fresh" Jesus and the Apostle Paul felt after walking many miles or riding a donkey to get to their meetings? I also wonder how "fresh" Joni Eareckson Tada feels when she gets to her meetings? She is a Christian author and speaker, who is also a quadriplegic. And, guess what Joyce? Joni has her own Christian ministry also, but Joni has never spent any of her ministry's funds on a private jet. And, although being a quadriplegic, Joyce, Joni endures those "hassles" at the airport on her way to her meetings. Furthermore, Joni won't even fly "first class", but rather flies "business class", because it is half the price, and she wants to be faithful with her ministry's funds. Joni doesn't just *talk* the gospel of Christ, Joyce, Joni also *walks* the gospel of Christ.

What a contrast between these prosperity preachers and the Apostle Paul, who said, in 1st

Corinthians 9:18, that he presented the gospel "without charge", so that he *did not abuse his authority* in the gospel. Obviously, today's prosperity preachers are **not** presenting the gospel "without charge", and *are abusing their authority in the gospel.*

Keep in mind that all of these mega church pastors and prosperity preachers talk a lot about the importance of Christians faithfully paying their 10% tithe. Because of this heavy emphasis on tithing, tens of millions of "tithe dollars" come into these churches and ministries every month. The tithe is supposed to be used for gospel ministry. But, as you can see, many millions of these "tithe dollars" are being spent on private jets, luxury yachts, multimillion dollar homes, "fat cat" CEO type preachers' salaries, and multiple luxury automobiles costing hundreds of thousands of dollars. The Bible is clear that the tithe is "God's money", not a *slush fund* for prosperity preaching "hucksters" to dip into so they can surround themselves with worldly pleasures and treasures.

Chapter Three

Prosperity Gospel Heresy and Blasphemy

A m I "out of line" for *calling out* these preachers and *exposing* their lavish lifestyles, their misuse of God's tithe dollars, and their false teachings? Am I sowing "discord" among the brethren? Is my labeling them as **hucksters** "over the top" and harsh? All of these questions will be answered in the following paragraphs.

In Ephesians 5:11, the Apostle Paul states that we are to **expose the works of darkness**. So, part of our responsibility as Christians is to expose darkness. These preachers are manipulating and twisting God's Holy Scriptures, deceiving millions of people, and abusing God's tithe funds by misappropriating them to pay for "worldly toys". So, per the Apostle Paul, *they must be exposed*.

In 2nd Timothy 4:2, Paul stated that we need to be ready to convince, *rebuke* and exhort. And, Paul goes on to say, in 1st Timothy 4:3-4, that the reason we need to do so is because the time will come when they will not endure "sound doctrine", but instead will be turned away from the truth, and will be turned to *fables*. As is revealed in this book, that time is here. Therefore, per the Apostle Paul, those proclaiming these false doctrines need to be "rebuked". The prosperity gospel is certainly one of those "fables" being taught, and, therefore, those proclaiming it are to be rebuked.

Paul also states, in 1st Timothy 5:19-20, that "elders" who sin are to be rebuked in the "presence of all"; in other words, they are to be rebuked **publicly**. (Note: This passage does also say not to receive an accusation against an elder without two or three witnesses, which I will discuss in the next paragraph). Elders, of course, are church leaders. I think it is fair to say that these famous preachers I've mentioned by name, with their nationwide ministries, are certainly church leaders as well. So, once again, per the Apostle Paul, *these preachers must be rebuked*

publicly. And, we have a couple of biblical examples of the Apostle Paul himself doing just that; publicly calling people out by name whose teachings or behavior contradicted Scripture. In 2nd Timothy 2:16-18, Paul called out Hymenaeus and Philetus by name for falsely teaching that the resurrection was already passed, which Paul said overthrew the faith of some. Paul also publicly rebuked the Apostle Peter in his letter to the Galatians, in Galatians 2:11-14. In this passage, Paul basically called Peter a "hypocrite".

Now, I do need to mention that, in the 1st Timothy 5:19-20 passage, it began by saying not to receive accusations against an "elder" without there being at least two or three witnesses to attest to the accuracy of the accusations. Well, I can provide you with more witnesses than that. If you go to Google and do a name search for the preachers I've mentioned by name, you will find numerous individuals and organizations with YouTube videos, websites, and/or blogs bearing witness to the accusations levied at these impostors in this book. You will find dozens of verifiable accounts of their compromises, falsehoods, blasphemies and heresies. All that you need to do is to type their first and last name into the search bar along with the word "heresy" or the words "false teacher", and you will find an abundance of evidence. You will be able to pull up videos and/or audio recordings of these preachers saying alarming, outlandish and heretical things.

You will be able to hear Joyce Meyer say that Jesus was *"born again in Hell"* during the time between His burial and resurrection. I ask Joyce to please give me the specific scripture that specifically states that Jesus was *"born again in Hell"*. However, Joyce will not be able to give me that scripture because it does not exist. You will also be able to hear Meyer say that Jesus was thrown to the "floor" in Hell and all the demons of Hell were jumping on Jesus' back. I did not know that Hell has a "floor". And, I am still looking for that scripture with the demons jumping on Jesus' back as well. However, once again, that scripture does not exist. You will be able to hear Joyce Meyer say that she is *not a sinner*. Joyce goes on to say that it would be a lie from the "pit of hell" for her to say that she is a sinner. However, the Apostle Paul, who God used to write about half of the New Testament, stated in 1st Timothy 1:15: "This is a faithful saying and worthy of all acceptance, that Christ Jesus came into the world to save *sinners*, of whom *I am chief*." Church historians agree that the books of 1st and 2nd Timothy were written towards the end of Paul's life. He had already been preaching the gospel for at least 25 years. And yet, this mighty apostle still referred to himself as a *sinner*; in fact, as the "chief" of sinners. And, don't let Joyce try to bamboozle you by saying that Paul was referring to his past life before he came to Christ. Paul did not say, "of whom I *was* chief". Paul said, "of whom I *am* chief", present tense. So who are you going to believe, Joyce Meyer or the Apostle Paul?

As you continue your Google search, you can hear Kenneth Copeland say that heaven is a "planet". And, you will be able to hear Kenneth Copeland say that God is six feet and two or three inches tall, and weighs about 200 pounds. Copeland also says that God's hand measures nine inches from His extended thumb to the end of His little finger. Where does Copeland get this hand measurement for God? In Isaiah 40:12, God states that He has measured heaven with a "span". And, because the Webster's Dictionary defines the word "span" as being approximately nine inches, because it is the distance between the extended thumb and the end of the little finger of an average human hand; therefore, Copeland jumps to the outlandish conclusion that this "human span" must also apply to God's hand. I encourage you to read Isaiah 40:12. It says that "God's span" is big enough to measure heaven. Well, if Copeland is right about the size of God's hand, then heaven is only nine inches long. And, this verse in Isaiah also says that God's hand can hold the waters, presumably of the Earth. Well, once again, if Copeland is right about God's nine inch hand, there must only be about a half a cup of water on this Earth, because that is about all that a nine inch hand could hold. This verse in Isaiah also says that God can weigh all the mountains of Earth in scales. I don't think that Copeland's six foot tall, 200 pound God would be able to do that. Copeland's "god" is **not** the God of the Holy Bible. Copeland's god is a small god, not much bigger than Copeland. The God of the Bible measures the vast universe with His hand, and can hold all the waters of the oceans, seas, lakes and rivers on this planet in the palm of His hand. The God of the Bible can be seated on His throne in Heaven while His feet are simultaneously resting on His "footstool" of this Earth, per Matthew 5:34-35 and Acts 7:49. The God of the Bible's presence is not limited to a six foot tall body; the God of the Bible's presence is everywhere simultaneously. As David said in Psalm 139:7-10, if he ascends to Heaven, God is there; if he makes his bed in Hell, God is there, if he takes wings and flies to the uttermost parts of the sea, God is there. Kenneth Copeland's six foot tall god is **not** the God of the Bible. We will see if Copeland still has the same assessment of God on judgement day.

You will also be able to hear Kenneth Copeland say: "When I read in the Bible where He (God) says "I AM", *I just smile and say, yes, I AM too*". That's right, Kenneth Copeland also claims to be "I AM". This is an overt blasphemous statement by Copeland. You can hear Kenneth Copeland say that God is the *biggest failure* in the Bible, but, per Copeland, the only difference between Him and us is that God does not call Himself a failure. Copeland then explains why he makes this assertion. He says it is because God lost His top ranking angel, Lucifer; God lost the first man and the first woman He created; God lost the whole Earth; and because God also lost one-third of the angels. When Copeland says that God is a failure because of these "losses" that Copeland mentioned, then Copeland is asserting that these "losses" were God's fault. Think about it; Copeland is literally taking the side of the devil, because he is saying that it was God's fault that Lucifer and one-third of the angels fell. Copeland will have the opportunity to discuss this statement with God on judgement day as well.

You will be able to hear Kenneth Copeland say that the Protestant Reformation of 500 years ago was a "church split" that was in the hands of *wicked spirits*. And, per Copeland, the longer that "protest" (the Protestant Reformation) went on, *the more strength Satan gained*. Copeland stated that when representatives from the Catholic and Lutheran churches signed a document on October 31, 1999, which stated that both churches agreed that justification is attained by grace through faith in Jesus Christ alone, thus ending the "protest" over how a person is justified; Copeland stated that when that happened, that *church demon*, the "protest", the Protestant Reformation, had fallen. Copeland declared, "*that separating spirit of division*", the Protestant Reformation, had been pulled down.

It seems there are no limitations to Kenneth Copeland's arrogance, complete biblical ignorance, blasphemies, heresies and outright Satanic statements. The Protestant Reformation was **not** a "church split". It was the complete abandonment of an evil Catholic Church that was selling forgiveness in the form of indulgences, calling the Pope another god on earth, stating that all the names that apply to Christ also apply to the Pope, declaring that the Pope had authority to modify and abrogate divine laws, proclaiming that the Pope had the power to "dispense with" (get rid of) the laws of Christ, forbidding the common people to have a Bible, and burning Christians at the stake for owning a Bible and for teaching their children the Lord's Prayer or the Ten Commandments. The Catholic Church had in fact already burned millions of sincere Christians at the stake by the time of Martin Luther and the Protestant Reformation. In spite of this, Copeland takes the side of the Catholic Church, who committed these atrocities, and states that this Protestant Reformation was *in the hands of wicked spirits*, and that the longer the Protestant Reformation continued *the more strength Satan gained*. Well, I have news for you, Kenneth Copeland. It was not the Protestant reformers, who were martyred by the millions for their faith in Christ and for their love for the Scriptures, who were in the hands of *wicked spirits*. Rather, it is you, Kenneth Copeland, the self-proclaimed "I AM", who is in the hands of wicked spirits. And, the Protestant Reformation was not a "*church demon*" that, per Copeland, had fallen on October 31, 1999. If there is a "church demon" it is Kenneth Copeland himself, who calls God the biggest failure in the Bible, refers to himself as "I AM", and who tries to bring God down to the size of a man. Satan did not become stronger the longer the Protestant Reformation continued, but Satan does become stronger every time Kenneth Copeland opens his mouth and spews his heresies and blasphemous statements. Satan does become stronger with each and every dollar of God's "holy tithes" that Copeland spends on his fleet of private jets and airplanes, his fleet of luxury automobiles, his private airport, and on his 18,000 square foot, $6 million mansion. How dare this multimillionaire huckster, blasphemer and heretic accuse these men and women of God who paid the ultimate price, being burned alive at the stake, for their faith in Christ and in His Scriptures; how dare Copeland state that they were in the hands of wicked spirits and giving strength to Satan. Kenneth Copeland, you have no fear of God, but you will on judgement day.

As previously mentioned, Copeland also stated that, when the Lutheran and Catholic churches signed that document on October 31, 1999, "that *separating spirit of division* (the Protestant Reformation) was pulled down". It seems as though Copeland cannot think of enough ways to denounce the Protestant Reformation. We've already discussed Copeland calling it a "demon", and stating that *it was in the hands of wicked spirits and strengthened Satan.* Now, because Protestants separated and divided themselves from the Catholic Church during the Protestant Reformation, Copeland calls it a "separating spirit of division".

You could almost feel sorry for Copeland's total and complete ignorance of Scripture, while trying to be a Bible preacher and teacher, if it wasn't for the fact that Copeland's statements are so blasphemous, heretical and downright wicked. Copeland's statement of, "that separating spirit of division has been pulled down", obviously indicates that, "the Protestants' separating themselves from the Catholic Church", was an evil thing in Copeland's mind; moreover, that "division" is always an evil thing. Apparently, Copeland does not spend much time reading the Gospels, or he would have noticed Jesus' statement in Luke 12:51, where Jesus said: "Do you suppose that I came to give peace on earth? I tell you, not at all, but rather *division.*" This world's systems and Satanic influences are at enmity with Jesus Christ and His Holy Scriptures. There is no accord between them. So, Christians must "divide" or "separate" themselves from the things of this world and from all Satanic influences. In Ephesians 5:11, the Apostle Paul states that we are not to have fellowship with the works of darkness, but rather are to *expose* them. And, in 2nd Corinthians 6:14-17, Paul asks, "What fellowship has righteousness with wickedness or lawlessness? What communion has light with darkness? What accord has Christ with Belial (Satan)?" And, the obvious answer to these questions is "**none**". There can be no fellowship, agreement, accord or communion between the forces of Satan's darkness and wickedness, with Christ's forces of light and righteousness. And, that's why verse 17 in this passage follows with the Lord's command to "*come out from among them and be separate*".

Now I ask you, isn't that exactly what the Protestants did during the Protestant Reformation? They obeyed Ephesians 5:11 and determined to have no more fellowship with the works of darkness in the Catholic Church, and instead exposed these works of darkness during the Protestant Reformation. They obeyed 2nd Corinthians 6:14-17 and determined to have no more fellowship or communion with the wickedness, darkness and Satanic influences in the Catholic Church, and obeyed the Lord's command to come out of this evil church and to separate themselves from it. Remember, that the Catholic Church in the Middle Ages had become totally evil, filled with wickedness and darkness, and totally under the influence of Satan. As previously mentioned, the Catholic Church was selling forgiveness in the form of indulgences, calling the Pope another god on Earth, stating that all the names that apply to Christ also apply to the Pope, declaring that the Pope had authority to modify and abrogate divine laws, proclaiming that the Pope had the power to "dispense with" (get rid of) the laws of Christ, forbidding the common people to have a Bible, and burning Christians at the stake for owning a Bible and for teaching their children the Lord's Prayer or the Ten Commandments. By the time of Martin Luther and the Protestant Reformation, the Catholic Church had already burned millions of sincere Christians at the stake. And so, these faithful and obedient Protestant Christians, who had already been slaughtered by the millions by the Catholic Church, obeyed Jesus' word and came out from that wicked, dark, satanically influenced organization.

You see, Kenneth Copeland, the Protestant Reformation was **not** a "separating spirit of division", but rather was obedience to God's Word, as has been proven. Of course, obedience to God's Word is something that Kenneth Copeland knows very little about. Multiplied millions of these Protestant Reformers spilled their blood for their faith in Jesus Christ, while being burned alive at the stake; only to have this puny, ignorant and evil man, this blasphemer and heretic, Kenneth Copeland, accuse them of being a "demon" and strengthening Satan. If you support Kenneth Copeland's ministry, you are supporting heresy and blasphemy, and you will give account on judgement day.

When you do your Google search, you can also hear Creflo Dollar say that Adam could "transport himself", and that he could *fly*. I'm also still trying to find this scripture; perhaps it is in 1st "Crefalonians". Evidently Creflo and Joyce Meyer must have attended the same theology school, and both of them apparently study the "**Bozo**" translation of the Bible. You can also hear Creflo say that every sinner who "tithes" ends up being saved. Creflo loves those tithe dollars. The biblically correct statement is, "every sinner who places their faith in Jesus Christ as their Savior, and surrenders their life to Jesus as their Lord, will be saved". As you continue your Google search, you will hear Creflo say, "The Bible *is all about money*". However, Jesus said that the Scriptures are all about Him, in John 5:39. You will hear Creflo Dollar say that, "you need money, or you will never have peace". Once again, I ask Creflo to please show me the scripture which states that. My Bible says that Jesus Christ is the "Prince of Peace", that Jesus Christ is our peace, and that we will have "perfect peace" if we keep our minds focused on Him, per Isaiah 9:6, Ephesians 2:14 and Isaiah 26:3. The Scriptures are clear that, if you have Jesus, you have peace, whether you are financially rich or poor. Creflo's statement is not only biblically inaccurate, it is heretical. The Bible says, "Jesus brings peace"; Creflo says, "money brings peace". Did you notice that in all three of the previous statements by Creflo, he replaces "Jesus" with "money"? The Bible says *Jesus* brings salvation; Creflo says *paying tithes (money)* brings salvation. The Bible says that the Scriptures are all about *Jesus*; Creflo says that the Bible is all about *money*. The Bible states that *Jesus* brings peace; Creflo states that *money* brings peace. In every case Creflo replaces "Jesus", who is God, with the word "money". Why? I would suggest that if a person consistently replaces Jesus/God with *money*, it is probably because their god is money.

You can also hear Creflo Dollar say that Jesus was **not** God on Earth. Do you notice a pattern here? Once again Jesus is the "target" of Creflo's false and heretical teaching. Was Jesus still God when He was on this Earth? Matthew 1:23 states that, "they shall call His name Immanuel, which is translated, *God with us*". 1st Timothy 3:16 says that, "*God* was manifested in the flesh". In John 5:18, John said that, "Jesus made Himself *equal with God*". In John 8:58, Jesus declared Himself to be "*I AM*"; the name God used to identify Himself when He appeared to Moses in the burning bush. And, in John 20:24-29, when Thomas called Jesus, "**My Lord and my God**", Jesus did not correct him, but rather, Jesus said to him, "Thomas, because you have seen me you have believed. Blessed are those who have not seen and yet have believed". So, in this passage, Jesus acknowledges Thomas' belief in Him as "*Lord and God*", and then Jesus pronounced a blessing on those who come to this belief in Him without ever having seen Him.

As you proceed with your Google search, you will be able to hear Jesse Duplantis say that he went to Heaven in a type of "cable car or chariot". And, Jesse describes in vivid detail the conversations he had in Heaven, and the things that were told him in Heaven. I find that interesting and quite contradictory when compared to the Apostle Paul's experience when he was caught up to the *third heaven*, which Paul also referred to as "Paradise", in 2nd Corinthians 12:1-4. Paul said that, when he was in Heaven, the things he heard there were "inexpressible", and were ***not lawful for a man to utter***. I'm thinking that Jesse went to a different "heaven" than the one that Paul went to. In Jesse's testimony regarding his trip to Heaven, Jesse also refers to the statement in the book of Revelation about "tears being wiped away". Jesse states that he has been "shown" that this does not apply to redeemed human beings, but that it refers to the tears in Jesus' eyes being wiped away. However, my Bible states, in Revelation 21:4, that "God will wipe away every tear from ***their*** eyes", not from Jesus' eyes. This verse is clearly and unarguably referring to God wiping away the tears from the eyes of the redeemed, not from the eyes of Jesus. So, once again Jesse is caught contradicting Scripture. In Jesse's account of his supposed time in Heaven, he also states that Jesus was crying, so Jesse said that he, Jesse, reached out and touched Jesus and *"comforted" Jesus*. I did not know that Jesse is the "comforter", I always thought that the comforter was the Holy Spirit, as well as God the Father and Jesus Christ. I am quite sure that if any comforting will be done in Heaven, it will be Jesus, the Holy Spirit, and God the Father doing the comforting of redeemed humans, not humans comforting any members of the Godhead. I also find it surprising that Jesse was still "standing" when the "post resurrection and ascension" *glorified* Jesus Christ *supposedly* met him in Heaven. When the "post resurrection and ascension" *glorified* Jesus appeared to the Apostle John, in Revelation 1:12-17, John fell at Jesus' feet as though dead. Likewise, when the Apostle Paul shares his Damascus Road experience with King Agrippa, in Acts 26:12-15, Paul states that, when Jesus appeared to him, there was a light that accompanied Jesus' presence that was brighter than the sun, and Paul states that he, as well as all of those with him, fell to the ground, which is similar to John's experience recorded in Revelation. But not the mighty

Jesse Duplantis; Jesse is not knocked to the ground. I'm thinking that Jesse met a different Jesus than the Jesus who Paul and John met.

When conducting your Google search, you can also hear Jesse say that God did not know what He had created when He created the animals, as recorded in the book of Genesis. Per Jesse, God had to ask Adam what He, God, had created. And, Jesse goes on to say that Adam was the one who actually brought the animals to life. Jesse states that God had just created animal "mannequins", with no life in them. Jesse also said that God then said to Adam, "speak spirit", and when Adam gave each animal a name, then they would come to life.

There is just one problem with Jesse's account. It is not in the Bible. There is no Bible verse which states that God did not know what He had created. There is no Bible verse which states that God just created lifeless "mannequins" when He created the animals. There is no Bible verse which states that God said "speak spirit" to Adam. There is no Bible verse which states that the animals came to life as Adam named them. Jesse is obviously reading that same "**Bozo**" translation used by Creflo and Joyce. The account in Genesis 2:19-20 simply states that God allowed Adam to choose the names for each animal.

There are two "key words" used in Genesis 2:19-20, which describe what Adam's role was in regard to the animals. These key words are "call/called" and "name/names". These verses state that God brought the animals to Adam to see what Adam would "call" them. And, whatever Adam "called" them was its "name". It then goes on to state that Adam gave "names" to all. The Hebrew word translated as call or called is "qara", and the Hebrew word translated as name or names is "shem".

So, according to Genesis 2:19-20, Adam did two things in regard to the animals. He *qara*, "called", the animals *shem*, "names". And, guess what? Neither of these original Hebrew words, "qara" or "shem", which describe what Adam did regarding the animals, are ever translated as spirit, breathed, living, life or created; not even once in the entire Bible. In other words, what Adam did regarding the animals had nothing whatsoever to do with creating life or spirit, giving life or spirit, or breathing life or spirit into the animals. What these Hebrew words are simply saying is that Adam gave the animals their names, period.

Furthermore, the animals were already revealed to be alive in Genesis chapter one before God ever brought them to Adam to give them their names in Genesis chapter two. In Genesis 1:20, on the fifth day of creation, God said "let the water abound with *living* creatures and let the birds *fly* above the earth". And, this was before Adam was even created. Have you ever seen "lifeless mannequin birds" fly? I'm pretty sure these birds were *alive* if they were flying on the fifth day of creation in Genesis chapter one. Then, in Genesis 1:24, God again said to let the earth bring forth the "*living*" creature regarding the land animals. And, this also was before Adam had been created. All of these animals were created *alive* before God ever created Adam. God did not need Adam to give life to the animals. God is the "life giver", not Adam.

Jesse's statements regarding Adam and the creation of the animals are so outlandish, biblically ignorant and heretical that it takes your breath away. Jesse may be a good comedian, but he is an extremely shallow and often heretical Bible teacher.

I encourage you to read Job chapters 38 thru 41 regarding God's creation, where God speaks in detail about many of the animals that He created, such as the bear and its cubs, the wild mountain goats and deer and their offspring, the wild donkey and the wild ox, the ostrich and the stork, the hawk and the eagle, the horse, the behemoth, and leviathan. And, God asks Job, "were you there when I created these things?" I am quite sure that God would have much stronger language for Jesse. At least Job had never asserted that God did not even know what He had created when He created the animals, or that Adam was the one who gave life to the animals. I think that God will also want to discuss a few things with Jesse on judgement day, just as with Jesse's good friend Kenneth Copeland.

Finally, via your Google search, you can hear Benny Hinn, Kenneth Copeland, Jesse Duplantis, Creflo Dollar and Joyce Meyer say that they are "gods". This is straight out of the "New Age" religion. New Age teachers have been saying for decades that human beings are "gods".

These prosperity preaching "gods" refer to Psalm 82:6, where God states: "I said you are gods". When you read the full chapter in Psalm 82, it is clear that this "title" was referring to the "judges" of Israel who were serving and representing God among the people. God was certainly **not** creating a new "doctrine" in this chapter which teaches us that human beings are "gods".

These preachers also refer to John 10:34-35 where Jesus cleverly quoted and used this passage, Psalm 82:6, when the Jews were ready to stone Him. The reason they wanted to stone Jesus was because, as the Jews put it, "You make Yourself God". So, Jesus quoted this Psalm, and then basically said to them: "So how can you stone Me for saying that I am the Son of God, when this scripture in Psalms calls you "gods". It is obvious that Jesus just quoted this Psalm to confound the Jews when they were about to stone Him. Jesus was **not** creating a new doctrine for the Church, exalting sinful human beings to the position of "gods".

If the Psalmist in the Old Testament, and Jesus in the New Testament, were creating a new doctrine, which taught that human followers of God are also "gods", surely some of the other Bible writers, prophets and apostles would have mentioned it.

Did you ever read where Daniel, Isaiah, Jeremiah, Ezekiel or any of the 12 "minor prophets" in the Old Testament claimed to be "gods", or stated that people in general were "gods"? None of these Old Testament men of God ever made such a claim.

Did you ever read in the New Testament where Matthew, Mark, Luke, John, James, Peter, Jude, or the Apostle Paul claimed to be "gods", or declared that human beings in general were "gods"? None of these New Testament men of God ever made such a claim either.

It is only these multimillionaire, heresy spewing hucksters in the "prosperity gospel movement" who claim to be "gods". And, unfortunately, Kenneth Copeland, Creflo Dollar, Jesse Duplantis, Joyce Meyer and Benny Hinn are not the only ones making such claims to be "gods". There is a new younger generation of heretic preachers arising who are making similar claims. Perhaps the most well-known of these younger preachers is Steven Furtick. When you do your Google searches you will be able to pull up a video clip of Furtick where he states: "**I am God Almighty**". This, of course, is outright blasphemy. This is what Satan said when he was still known as Lucifer in Heaven. He also claimed that he would be God Almighty. Anyone who is a follower of Steven Furtick, and financially contributes to his ministry, as well as the ministries of Copeland, Dollar, Duplantis, Meyer and Hinn, *is financing heresy and blasphemy*.

You can also pull up a video where Steven Furtick compares the resurrection of Jesus Christ to the "zombies" being alive from the dead in the television program titled, "The Walking Dead". In this video Furtick speaks of having watched all of the seasons of this program about zombies, which is troubling in itself, and Furtick tells his audience:

"Don't send me a thing about the Word of God and "The Walking Dead". It's in the Bible: the "walking dead"; third day, Jesus Christ, Lazarus, the "SAME STUFF."

Once again, this is outright blasphemy and heresy, to compare Jesus Christ's being raised to life from the dead by Almighty God, to the zombies being alive from the dead in this secular television program, calling it the "**same stuff**". Furtick is certainly a worthy blasphemous heretic replacement for the older generation of blasphemers and heretics, Copeland, Duplantis, Dollar etc..

It makes you wonder why so many pastors open their pulpits to these teachers of heresy. I mention this because much of these false teachers' income is from flying throughout our nation in their private jets to speaking engagements in Pentecostal and charismatic mega churches across America. Why are they willing to fly their jets to these speaking engagements? It is because the pastors of these churches take up an extremely generous offering for them at each of these events. I attended such an event back in 1997 or 1998 at a relatively small church, where the attendance at the meeting was only around 500 to 600 people. The prosperity speaker that night was Jesse Duplantis. Jesse promised that God would bring a hundredfold return to the people sowing a financial seed in his ministry that night. I thought it was a little odd, but they took the time to count the offering that night and publicly announced how much had been given. The offering amount that night was a little over $40,000, and that was at a meeting with only several hundred in attendance. Therefore, you can be sure that when Jesse Duplantis, Kenneth Copeland, Creflo Dollar, Benny Hinn, Steven Furtick, or Joyce Meyer have a speaking engagement at a large mega church with a few thousand attending, the amount of their offering is probably in the hundreds of thousands of dollars. Why would any pastor who is "biblically sound" and who has "spiritual discernment" allow these *peddlers of false teaching and heresy* into his pulpit, and allow them to financially *fleece his flock* by taking up an offering for them? Why would he allow his church members to become partners with these false teachers by financing their biblical falsehoods and heresies? There are only a few possible answers to that question. Either the pastor is severely biblically challenged, or he has no spiritual discernment, or he agrees with their unbiblical and heretical teachings. Whichever of these options it is, should be deeply concerning to all of those who attend that pastor's church. If the church you attend invites any of these "hucksters" to speak and take up offerings at your church, *you need to depart from your church;* you do not want to be a financial partner of such an organization.

What about my "labeling" these preachers as *hucksters*? Am I out of line regarding that? I encourage you to read Isaiah 56:9-11, where God's unfaithful religious leaders/shepherds are referred to as blind watchmen, "dumb dogs" and as *greedy* dogs. Why as "greedy" dogs? This passage explains why. It says that they "never have enough" and that their focus is on their "own gain". Does this not accurately describe today' prosperity preachers? They start with one luxury car, but it's not enough, until they end up with several luxury cars. They start with one private jet, but it's not enough, so they get a second private jet. They start with one multimillion dollar home, but it's not enough, so they get a second luxurious and expensive home. And, as this passage said, it is all for their "own gain". These verses in Isaiah are similar to what the prophet Ezekiel wrote in Ezekiel 34:1-2, where God said: "Woe to the shepherds of Israel who *feed themselves*! Should not the shepherds feed the flock?" And, in Ezekiel 34:8, God said again that the shepherds *fed themselves* instead of feeding the flock. Once again, this is exactly what prosperity preachers are doing as they receive tithe dollars dedicated to God, and then spend these sacred funds on Rolex watches, diamond rings, designer clothing, luxury automobiles, yachts, private jets, and pastoral mansions.

I also encourage you to read Matthew 23:13-33 and John 8:44. In these passages, you will hear Jesus call the false religious leaders and teachers of His day, "hypocrites, fools, serpents, vipers, and children of the devil". These names are a bit harsher than the term *huckster* that I use. I likewise encourage you to read Galatians 2:11-14 and 2nd Corinthians 11:13-15. In these scriptures, you will hear the Apostle Paul call Peter a "hypocrite" in the Galatians passage, and, in the Corinthians text, you will hear Paul call the false religious leaders in the Corinthian Church: false apostles, deceitful workers, and *Satan's ministers*. Once again, these names, which include the terms hypocrite and "Satan's ministers", are a bit more harsh than the word *huckster* that I use. And, as previously documented, this term "huckster" is used in the Amplified Bible and in the Strong's Expanded Exhaustive Concordance, to describe those who "peddle" the Word of God. So, I have good company regarding the usage of this word.

So, as you can see, what I am doing in this book is **not** *sowing discord*, otherwise Isaiah, Ezekiel, the Apostle Paul and Jesus Christ would also have been guilty of sowing discord when they also exposed and "labeled" the false religious leaders of their day. What I am doing in this book is following the example of Isaiah, Ezekiel, the Apostle Paul and Jesus regarding dealing with false religious teachers and leaders, by exposing them publicly, and also by selecting the "correct label" that accurately describes them. For the false religious leaders in Isaiah's and Ezekiel's time, the correct labels were "blind watchmen, dumb dogs, greedy dogs, and shepherds who feed themselves instead of feeding the flock". For the false religious leaders that Jesus was exposing, the correct labels were "fools, hypocrites, serpents, vipers, and children of the devil". For the false religious leaders in the Corinthian Church that Paul was exposing, the correct labels were "false apostles, deceitful workers, and Satan's ministers". And, for the prosperity preachers that I am exposing, the correct label is "hucksters".

The Bible has warned us, in 2nd Peter 2:1-3, that false teachers would arise teaching heresies and exploiting Christians with deceptive words for *covetous purposes*; and, in 1st Timothy 6:3-5, stating that those who teach unscriptural things and who use "godliness" (the things of God) as a means of personal gain, are proud and have corrupt minds that are destitute of the truth. In 1st Timothy 6:5, the Apostle Paul said to *withdraw yourself* from teachers such as these.

1st Timothy 6:7-8 reminds us that we came into this world without any material possessions, and that we will not be able to take any with us when we leave, so we should be content with just having food and clothing. Does that sound anything like today's prosperity gospel? Absolutely not! Anyone who has read the Apostle Paul's letters and the Gospels of Matthew, Mark, Luke and John, as well as the Book of Acts, depicting the faithful, obedient, spirit filled, and "on fire" first century Christian Church, knows that today's prosperity preaching mega church brand of Christianity does not even remotely resemble the Christian Church revealed in the Bible. That first century Christian Church revealed in the Book of Acts and in the Apostle Paul's letters, was financially poor, but spiritually rich. That Church considered the world to be its "enemy", **not** its "friend". Today's 21st century prosperity preaching mega church brand of Christianity is financially rich, but spiritually bankrupt. Today's Church no longer considers the world to be its enemy; it loves the world and its worldly pleasures and treasures. And, if it does not repent and reform, the vast majority of professed Christians attending these prosperity preaching mega churches will **not** be ready for the return of Jesus, and will be "lost".

Chapter Four

Prosperity Gospel—Does Everyone Get Healed?

Remember that prosperity preachers not only promise *wealth* for having strong faith and sowing financial seeds into their ministries and mega churches; they also promise *good health*. These preachers say that "everyone" who has strong faith **will be healed**.

I find it interesting that the most famous of these "healing" prosperity preachers, Benny Hinn, when investigated by NBC Dateline, **could not medically prove even "one instance" where someone at his crusades had actually been healed**. And, one of Hinn's own bodyguards, when anonymously interviewed by NBC, stated that only people who can physically demonstrate that they are already healed are allowed up on stage at Hinn's crusades. The bodyguard went on to say that the seriously ill are ***never allowed on stage***.

In 2001 a documentary about Hinn's healing claims was done by HBO. It was titled, "A Question of Miracles". This documentary followed the lives of seven people who had supposedly been healed at a Benny Hinn crusade; they were followed for one year. At the end of the year, the film director, Anthony Thomas, concluded that ***none*** of them had actually been healed.

One of the prosperity preachers mentioned by name earlier in this book, who has always stated that everyone with strong faith gets healed, was himself called out on a national radio broadcast a number of years ago for having flown to another country in his private jet to obtain surgery for a medical condition, because he did not want his financial supporters to know that he also gets sick. And, the radio host publicly challenged this prosperity preacher to sue him if it was not true. Of course, there are no records of any lawsuits having been filed.

Whenever I've heard these prosperity preachers speak of their great faith, and assert that everyone with faith will be healed, I've always wondered why these preachers with their *supposed* "great faith" don't visit the children's cancer wards and heal all of these children; these little children are dying painful deaths from cancer, but not one of these "great men of faith" make an effort to heal them. Why not? After all, we've all heard preachers speak about the "faith of a child". So, between that simple and strong "faith of a child", combined with the "great faith" of these prosperity preachers, certainly all of these children would be healed, right? Why aren't these preachers visiting those cancer wards and healing those suffering children? I'll tell you why, because just as their *prosperity wealth* message is a "sham", even so their *prosperity health* message is a "sham" as well.

It is estimated that there are one million deaf people in America. There are also one million blind people. There are six million people who are paralyzed. 600,000 Americans die from cancer each year, and 655,000 die from heart disease. Where are all of the prosperity preaching "faith healers"? Instead of healing the deaf, blind, paralyzed, and those with terminal cancer and heart disease, as people who truly had the gift of healing did in the New Testament, these "fake healers" are adjusting legs that are allegedly a tiny bit shorter than the other. As you can see, it is indeed all a sham.

I do need to mention that I do believe in the gift of healing. It is biblical. I am not one of the dispensationalists who claim that the gift of healing, and the other spiritual gifts, were only for the time period of the original apostles. I believe they use that argument as a "loser's limp", because they don't want to admit that their own weak faith, lack of complete obedience, and lack of total surrender to Christ, is the problem. These spiritual gifts, including healing, are available for us today just as they were for first century Christians; the Bible is clear about this. The reason that we rarely see these gifts in today's Christian Church, is because we do not exercise the kind of strong faith that Christians did back then; we do not love as they did; we do not spend the amount of time in prayer, fellowship, and studying God's Word as they did; we do not fully obey God as they did; and we have not fully, 100% surrendered our lives to Christ as they did. I will not blame God for today's absence of these spiritual gifts, such as the gift of healing, as dispensationalists do, by saying that God does not offer these gifts anymore. As I said, this is dispensationalists' spiritual "loser's limp". I freely confess and admit that the problem is us, which includes me. It is our spiritual shortcomings that are limiting the flow of these mighty spiritual gifts from the Holy Spirit. The Scriptures are clear that God does not and has not changed. We have changed. We do not even remotely resemble the Christian Church of the first century. So, how can we expect to have the spiritual power and gifting of that Church.

Someday a great revival will take place among Christians throughout the world who are "all in" for Jesus, and these gifts will then appear again. And when they do, it will be the real thing. The deaf, the blind, the paralyzed, and those who are terminally ill will be healed.

Have you ever wondered why the Apostle Paul stated, in 2nd Timothy 4:20, that he had left Trophimus, who was one of Paul's fellow gospel ministers and traveling companions, in the town of Miletus because he was *sick*? Why didn't the great Apostle Paul heal Trophimus instead of leaving him behind *sick*? Do you think that Paul prayed for and healed everyone else, but did not pray for and attempt to heal his friend and fellow minister Trophimus? Or, did Paul and Trophimus, who risked their lives for the gospel, simply not have as great of faith as today's prosperity preachers? The answer is obvious, not everyone who prays and asks for healing gets healed.

And, what about Timothy? According to Philippians 2:19-22, Paul was probably closer to Timothy and trusted Timothy more than anyone, and yet Paul told Timothy, in 1st Timothy 5:23, to "use a little wine for your *stomach's sake* and your *frequent infirmities*". The Greek word translated as infirmities in this passage is "astheneia", which, according to the Strong's Exhaustive Concordance, means feebleness, malady, frailty, disease, sickness, weakness or infirmity. In other words, Paul is stating in this passage that Timothy was a frail and physically weak person who was frequently sick. But, rather than miraculously and supernaturally healing Timothy of his frailties, weaknesses and frequent sicknesses, Paul instead advised Timothy to drink a little wine to help Timothy's infirmities. Why didn't Paul heal him? Paul and Timothy were "super close" as friends and as fellow ministers of the gospel. As with Trophimus, do you think that Paul prayed for and healed everyone else, but did not pray for and attempt to heal Timothy, his best friend and fellow minister? Or, once again, did Paul and Timothy, who put their lives on the line for the gospel each and every day, simply not have as great of faith as today's prosperity preachers? Here also, the answer is obvious, not everyone who prays and asks for healing gets healed.

Then, there is the case of the Apostle Paul himself. Paul stated that a "thorn" in the flesh had been given to him, and he said that he had "pleaded with the Lord" three times to have it removed, per 2nd Corinthians 12:7-8. Because this passage regarding the great Apostle Paul, who God used to write half of the New Testament, creates serious problems for prosperity preachers who proclaim this "prosperity health doctrine" that *everyone with faith gets healed*; therefore, prosperity preachers insist that this "thorn" had nothing to do with physical health issues for Paul. However, once again, prosperity preachers find themselves clearly contradicting the Bible. The Greek word translated as "thorn" in this passage is *skolops*. And, according to Strong's Expanded Exhaustive Concordance, this word means a "bodily annoyance" or ***disability***. And, Strong's goes on to say that Paul's language used in 2nd Corinthians 12:7, indicates that his thorn was ***physical, painful and humiliating***. So, who do you want to believe, the Greek experts or prosperity preachers?

Furthermore, Paul himself identifies this "thorn" as being his *infirmities* in 2nd Corinthians 12:9. Immediately after Paul quotes Jesus as telling him that Jesus' grace was sufficient for him, and that Jesus' strength was made perfect in Paul's *weakness*; Paul then states that he will therefore boast in his *infirmities*. And, this is that same Greek word, "astheneia", used in 1st Timothy 5:23 for Timothy's infirmities, which Strong's Concordance stated means "feebleness, malady, frailty, disease, sickness, weakness or infirmity". So, Paul's "thorn", from a biblical original Greek language standpoint, is an "open and shut case". Paul had some type of physical sickness, disease, frailty or weakness that he prayed to Jesus about on three occasions asking for it to be removed/healed, but the Apostle Paul also did not get healed, just as Trophimus and Timothy did not get healed.

At this point, prosperity preachers point out that in the very next verse, 2nd Corinthians 12:10, Paul not only mentions his *infirmities* again, but also mentions reproaches, distresses and persecutions that he has suffered for Christ. They suggest that these "persecution type sufferings" were the thorn in Paul's flesh that he asked to be removed, despite the clear meaning of the Greek words used by Paul which contradict these preachers' explanation. However, based on Paul's other statements regarding suffering persecutions, tribulations or afflictions for Christ, this explanation by prosperity preachers once again contradicts Scripture. Paul is the one who stated, in 2nd Timothy 3:12, that "all" who live godly in Christ Jesus will suffer persecution. Paul is the one who, in 1st Thessalonians 3:1-4, encouraged the Thessalonians not to be shaken by afflictions for Christ, and reminded them that he had previously told them that they would suffer tribulation. Paul is the one who told the Philippians, in Philippians 1:29, that it is our privilege not only to believe in Christ, but also to suffer for His sake. And, Paul is also the one, in Colossians 1:24, who said that he *"rejoiced"* in his sufferings, and that he considered himself to be *"lacking"* in afflictions for Christ; in other words, Paul said that he had not suffered enough for Christ. So, for these prosperity preachers to suggest that Paul was praying for the "thorn of persecution type sufferings" to be removed from him, blatantly contradicts all of these statements by Paul. The scriptures I have cited make it clear that Paul was **not** praying for persecution or reproaches for Christ to be removed from him. Rather, these scriptures tell us that Paul himself expected persecution, reproaches and suffering for Christ; that he also told others to expect persecution, reproaches and suffering for Christ; that he considered it a privilege to suffer these things for Christ; that he rejoiced in suffering these things for Christ; and that he considered himself to not have suffered enough for Christ. Therefore, prosperity preachers who endorse this explanation that Paul was praying for the removal of the thorn of persecution type sufferings, are making Paul out to be a hypocrite and a liar. Paul was not repeatedly praying to the Lord to have persecution and reproaches removed from him, while at the same time telling other Christians to expect these things, to not be shaken by them, and to count them as a privilege. And, Paul was not telling the Colossians that he rejoiced in suffering these things, and even wanted more sufferings for Christ, while at the same time repeatedly asking the Lord to remove them. The Apostle Paul is not a hypocrite or a liar. It is the prosperity preachers, who repeatedly contradict the Bible, who are the hypocrites and liars.

The Bible is clear that the Apostle Paul had some type of physical infirmity, sickness, disease or weakness that Paul asked the Lord to heal him of on three occasions. However, Paul was not healed, just as Trophimus and Timothy were not healed. And, I can guarantee you that Paul, Trophimus and Timothy had more faith in their little fingers than these prosperity preachers have in their entire bodies.

In addition to their teaching, that everyone with faith gets healed, clearly contradicting Scripture, this false doctrine also results in adding extra torment upon those suffering from sickness. Those who are seriously ill are already experiencing physical pain and suffering. Then the prosperity preachers heap additional *spiritual* pain and suffering upon them by telling them that if they had strong faith they would be healed. So, because they are not healed, it indicates that their faith is deficient. Therefore, the end result of this false teaching is that those suffering from illness now have the added burden of knowing that, not only are they physically sick, but they are also *spiritually sick*, because their faith is too weak to receive the blessing of healing, which is available and guaranteed to everyone who has strong faith, according to these prosperity preachers.

It should be apparent that both the *prosperity wealth message* and the *prosperity health message*, proclaimed by prosperity preachers, are unbiblical shams and scams being proclaimed to make these preachers rich, as they always ask the poor and the sick to sow financial seeds into their ministries as a "step of faith" to bring about their financial and physical restoration. The Bible clearly refutes both of these false teachings.

I hope that you are as outraged as I am regarding this *false prosperity gospel* being proclaimed by prosperity preachers, and regarding the other financial abuses covered in this book. If you belong to a mega church, demand a detailed copy of the church budget that lists all salaries "individually", and a detailed listing of all church assets, including any luxury cars, airplanes, pastoral homes etc.. And, if your church has "sold out" to the things of this world, "get out" and join a different church. Also, if you have been contributing to any prosperity gospel ministries, your contributions have **not** been furthering the gospel; they have been paying for the lavish lifestyle of scripture manipulating *hucksters*, as the Amplified Bible and Strong's Expanded Exhaustive Concordance called them. Do you want your financial contributions to help the homeless and feed starving children, while also preaching the gospel to them? Or, do you want your financial contributions to buy private jets, luxury automobiles, Rolex watches, diamond rings, and multimillion dollar homes for prosperity preachers? Your money was given to you by God. How do you think He wants you to spend it?

Now that you know the truth, what will you do? Will you continue to support these prosperity preachers, or will you join me in exposing them? These con artists give Christianity a bad name. And, they siphon away hundreds of millions of tithe dollars each year, which could have been used to preach the gospel to the millions dying of starvation throughout the world, and to the hundreds of thousands of homeless Americans, while at the same time providing the food, shelter and medical care needed by them.

If you would like to contact me, I would be happy to hear from you. I do personally respond to every email I receive. My email address is Godormen@gmail.com.

ABOUT THE AUTHOR

My name is Henry Bechthold. I am a non-denominational Christian pastor. I have been preaching and teaching God's Word for the past forty years. The scriptural views and doctrines that I espouse come from my personal study of God's Word in the Bible. When it comes to biblical doctrine, the traditions and opinions of man are of no importance. I will take one plain "thus saith the Lord" over a thousand human and denominational traditions. I am of the same mindset of the disciples of Jesus, who told the unfaithful and disobedient religious leaders of their day that they "ought to obey God rather than men".

Feel free to contact me at GodorMen@gmail.com.

Made in the USA
Columbia, SC
27 September 2021

46289038R00041